EMBRACING
GOD'S GRACE

Strength to face
life's challenges

YOUTH WITH A MISSION

ZondervanPublishingHouse
Grand Rapids, Michigan

A Division of HarperCollinsPublishers

Contents

foreword
Close Encounters with the Living God

Welcome to the Living Encounters Bible study series! We created this unique study to help sincere seekers find a deeper revelation of God. Our God loves to be pursued. He wants us to know and love him more, and there's no better way to learn of his character and his ways than through his written Word.

The Living Encounters series offers exciting new ways for you to engage Scripture and apply its truth to your life. Through this series, each participant is encouraged into living encounters with God, his Spirit, his Word, his people, and his world.

Some elements of the study are drawn from teaching methods that have been used for decades in our Discipleship Training Schools. As our students encounter God, their perspective on life changes radically. The very truth of the Scripture connects them to the global picture, to God's heart for the peoples of the world. Therefore, the more they come to know God, the more they want to make him known.

The Living Encounters series is a wonderful Bible study tool for people of various levels of spiritual maturity. Its flexible, user-friendly format appeals to people with different learning styles and cultural perspectives. And when coupled with the teaching aids found in the Christian Growth Study Bible (Zondervan), the series is a highly effective way to draw new understanding and guidance from the Scriptures.

May this series bring you a whole new appreciation of our awesome God—and set you on the pathway to many living encounters!

—Loren Cunningham,
Founder of Youth With A Mission

Introducing Living Encounters

Did you ever hear about a person you'd never met—what he said, what he looked like, what he did—and then you met him, and somehow the picture you had formed in your mind didn't fit at all? For better or worse, you were confronted with reality! An "encounter" does not mean a secondhand report about a person or a situation; it means a face-to-face meeting. In an encounter, you meet a person, and your knowledge about him or her combines with and adapts to the living reality.

This is what "Living Encounters" is all about. You have read God's Word, the Bible, but there is a gap between what it says and what you experience. You know God's Spirit is alive and well, but life would be a lot simpler if he sat down beside you and gave you advice. You like people, but sometimes loving them seems impossible. And then there's the whole world out there—so full of need and suffering that you don't know how to even begin to help.

Living Encounters are more than an analysis of Bible passages or a tool for group discussion. They are to help you *meet* and adjust your life to God's Word, God's Spirit, God's people, and God's world. They are designed to challenge you not only to grasp truth but to live it out, to connect it to your personal world and to the larger world around you. As you apply yourself to these studies, you can expect exciting changes both in your thinking and in your lifestyle.

The Living Encounters series is versatile. Each guide is divided into six sessions and can be used within a small-group discussion in a church or on a college campus. However, the series is designed so that it is just as effective for individual study.

The guides are personal. They constantly lead you to ask, "What does this mean to me and how do I apply it in my own life?" Questions reveal needs and desires of the heart and invite you to embrace the promises, assurances, exhortations, and challenges of God's Word. As you respond, the Spirit of God will be responding to you, renewing your mind and transforming you more into the likeness of Jesus Christ — the ultimate goal of all Bible study.

The Features

Each session includes the following basic features.

Opening Vignette

To draw you into the topic at hand, each session opens with a thought-provoking narrative.

Preparing Heart and Mind

These questions open your heart and focus your mind on what God wants to say to you in the passage. If you are using Living Encounters in a group setting, we strongly encourage you to include this section during the first fifteen minutes of your discussion. Please realize, however, that the entire study will probably take about an hour and fifteen minutes. If you don't have that much time, then ask your group members to reflect on these questions before you meet together, and begin your discussion with the section, "Engaging the Text."

Setting the Stage

The background information found in this sidebar will help you better understand the context of the study.

Engaging the Text

This important section leads you through a Bible passage using inductive Bible study questions. The inductive method prompts you to observe, interpret, and apply the Bible passage with a variety of question styles:

- Observation questions will help you focus on what the Bible says.
- Interpretation questions will help you step into the world of the original readers to understand better what the passage meant to them.
- Application questions will help you to apply the truth to your heart and present circumstances.

Responding to God

In this section, you will receive suggestions that will help you focus your individual or group prayer time.

Punch Line

This brief sentence or verse will reinforce the theme of the session.

Taking It Further

This section is designed to be completed between studies to reinforce and further apply what you have learned. It offers a variety of suggestions for connecting what you have studied to your everyday life.

- **Connecting to Life:** a variety of activities to stimulate your personal growth and ministry to others.
- **Digging Deeper:** additional Scriptures to give a deeper and broader understanding of what the Bible says about the topic of the study.
- **Meditation:** a time to reflect more deeply on a specific verse or passage.
- **Personal Expression:** creative suggestions to help you process and apply what you've learned in the session.
- **World Focus:** an encouragement to look beyond your personal realm to the needs of our world.

Additional Features

In addition to the above, the guides contain a variety of optional features. All are designed to appeal to different learning styles and gifts and to encourage deeper integration of material into all of life. It is expected that you will choose whatever features you find most useful for each session. These optional features, found in articles throughout the sessions, include:

- **Gray boxed material:** often these will be devotional articles relevant to the study.
- **People of Impact:** a snapshot of the life of a person who models the principles studied.
- **People Profile:** a brief description of a people group that needs to be reached with the gospel.
- **Hot Topic:** a discussion starter to use with other group members to stimulate deeper thinking on a difficult subject.

Leader's Notes

Leader's notes for each session are provided at the back of each study guide.

Suggestions for Individual or Group Study

Preparing Heart and Mind

1. Ask the Lord for insight, wisdom, and grace to understand the Bible passage and apply it to your own life.
2. Choose one or more of the preparation questions and take time to think about it.

Engaging the Text

1. Read and reread the assigned Bible passage. You may find it helpful to have several different translations. A good, literal translation rather than a paraphrase is recommended, such as the *New International Version*, the *New American Standard Bible*, the *New Revised Standard Version*, and the *New King James Bible*. The questions in each study are based on the *New International Version*. A Bible dictionary can also serve you well for look-

ing up any unfamiliar words, people, places, or theological concepts. Commentaries, while having great value, are not part of this kind of study, which uses the inductive method.

2. The questions are designed to help you make observations, draw conclusions, and apply God's truth to your life. Write your answers in the space provided. Recording your observations and conclusions is an important step in any study process. It encourages you to think through your answers thoroughly, thus furthering the learning process.

3. Note the optional elements offered in the sidebars. These are designed to encourage greater understanding of the passage being studied.

4. Be aware of the continuous presence of the Lord throughout the process. You may want to stop and pray in the midst of your study. Be sure to end your study with a time of waiting, listening, and responding to the Lord in prayer.

5. Be willing to participate in the discussion. The leader of the group will not be lecturing; rather, he or she will be encouraging the members of the group to discuss what they have learned from the passage. The leader will be asking the questions that are found in this guide. Plan to share what God has taught you in your individual study time.

6. Stick to the passage being studied. Your answers should be based on the verses which are the focus of the discussion and not on outside authorities such as commentators or speakers (or the commentary notes in your study Bible!).

7. Be sensitive to other members of the group. Listen attentively when they share. You can learn a lot from their insights! Stick with the topic— when you have insights on a different subject, keep it for another time so the group is not distracted from the focus of the study.

8. Be careful not to dominate the discussion. We are sometimes so eager to share that we leave too little opportunity for others to contribute. By all means participate, but allow others to do so as well.

9. Expect the Holy Spirit to teach you both through the passage and through other members of the group. Everyone has a unique perspective that can broaden your own understanding. Pray that you will have an enjoyable and profitable time together.
10. The "Responding to God" section is the place where you pray about the topics you have studied. At this time you will invite the Holy Spirit to work these truths further into each of your lives. Be careful not to overlook this essential aspect of your time together.

Taking It Further

1. Identify other questions that arise through the study so that you can pursue them later.
2. Choose one or more of the activities to help you apply the principles in your life. These are optional activities to be done on your own after the Bible study session.

Leader's Notes

If you are the discussion leader or simply want further information, you will find additional suggestions and ideas for each session in the Leader's Notes in the back of this guide.

Embracing God's Grace: Strength to Face Life's Challenges

"Aagh, Saturday! Another dreaded weekend alone," Lisa moaned as she rolled out of bed. Cookie crumbs flew everywhere as she cast aside the sheet. She dragged herself across the room through the clutter of dishes, empty Coke cans, and last week's Sunday newspaper.

"That Bible must be somewhere," she muttered as she sifted through a pile of dirty clothes. It had been weeks since she had seen it. Hopelessness sapped her strength. She didn't know what exactly had contributed to this downhill slide. Was it her dad's sudden death, or the unpaid bills, or possibly the betrayal of her closest Christian friend? "Who cares anyway?" she mumbled, and gave up the search. That's when Dan, her non-Christian friend from work, called. He was trying once again to get a date. She had always put him off before, knowing he was interested in more than a casual friendship. He made it clear he wanted her. "Sure, eight o'clock will be fine," she said. *Why not?* she thought. She was desperate.

Lisa needs the grace of God. As Andrew Murray observed in *An Apostle's Inner Life*, grace is that free gift from him "that not only pardons and accepts but works in us each moment with its divine energy to will and to do what is well pleasing to him." Life is full of temptation. Fear, bitterness, hopelessness, and the like can harden our hearts. Sin can appear too powerful to resist. But God in his grace not only forgives us of our sin; he also enables us to resist Satan and live for him. If you, like Lisa, need to know freedom from regrets and fears, release from life's traps and a greater conviction of your value to God . . .

. . . then this study is for you!

RISING ABOVE
Ephesians 2:1–10

session
ONE

John never rests. He is driven to be constantly doing, always busy, fearful of what he might discover within if he ever stopped and listened to his heart. He became a Christian several years ago, when he was twenty-one. No one else in his family has come to know God yet.

Jenna craves attention, especially from men. She dresses accordingly. Her friends led her to Christ last year.

Bob rarely takes a risk, even if it is God who is inviting him to do so. His fear of failure is too strong. Though he hasn't realized it, that fear is his god. His whole family is Christian. He can't remember when he accepted Jesus as his Savior, but he grew up knowing he had.

> **How much more will those who receive God's abundant provision of grace ... reign in life through ... Jesus Christ.**
>
> **——ROMANS 5:17**

John, Jenna, and Bob are not abnormal Christians. They simply testify to the fact that "flesh" is present and active in the body of Christ. Even though God's Spirit is in these three, he is sometimes ignored. Instead, strong feelings rooted in wrong thinking form the basis of their choices. For example, believing the lie that "failure is deadly" leads to fear of failure, and that fear regularly affects the decisions Bob makes. The apostle Paul refers to this complex of feelings, lies, and habits as our "flesh." His letter to the Ephesians is written to help believers learn to walk according to the Spirit and thus to resist the flesh.

Grace, God's active presence in our hearts through his Spirit, is his solution to flesh. Our responsibility is simply to learn to keep on receiving the grace he freely offers. With that grace, we can resist temptation and rise above any situation!

- What are cravings and how are they satisfied?

- Paint a picture with words of someone striving for a cause.

- Why is it difficult for most people to receive a gift?

engaging the text

setting the stage

- The Talmud and Mishnah, books of Jewish Law, had meticulous instructions of what to do and not do in order to achieve acceptance from God.

- For Paul to gain "legalistic righteousness" (Philippians 3:6) and thus be found acceptable to God before he met Christ, he had to strive continually to obey all these Jewish laws.

- Most of the Ephesian believers came from Gentile (non-Jewish) backgrounds. Generally, people in this culture had no concept of the one true God and they indulged freely in such things as sexual immorality, greed, and idolatry.

- The attempt of individuals to meet their most basic needs for identity and purpose apart from what God freely gives is called "flesh" in the Bible ("sinful nature" in the NIV).

- Paul clarifies further that flesh is rooted in wrong desires of the body and the mind (Ephesians 2:3).

Read Ephesians 2:1–10

1. Using this passage, describe the essential difference between a Christian and a non-Christian. (Include the difference on what each life produces.)

2. Paul states that before the Ephesians were Christians they "followed the ways of this world" (v. 2). What kind of actions or attitudes do you think Paul has in mind? In other words, what drove them? (See also Setting the Stage.)

3. In verse 3, Paul indicates that he too was once driven by his thoughts and desires, yet he was a "good Jewish boy," not a pagan. (See Setting the Stage.) What do you think drove him before he became a Christian? Explain why his flesh was just as evil as the flesh of the Gentiles.

Activating Faith

All the members of his family gathered around Mark's hospital bed as he took his last breath. Neither they nor the best doctors in the world could save him. Death was just too powerful.

Apart from God's power, there is no greater force in the world than death. All of us were spiritually dead (separated from God) until we (Christians) were made alive in Christ. The only way out of spiritual death is the gospel of Jesus Christ.

The gospel refers to God's actions in history, when his Son Jesus came to this earth as a tiny baby, lived an obedient life, and chose to die on the cross, paying the price for humanity's sin. Thus Jesus broke the power of death and was resurrected to offer new life, God's life, to all who choose to believe that he did this for them.

The unrelenting power of physical death from the dreadful disease called cancer won the battle for Mark's body, but death had lost its sting. Because of his faith in the gospel of Jesus Christ, Mark was full of resurrection life. He simply shed his outer shell, free at last to be with Jesus entirely. That's the power of the gospel.

It takes a choice to become a Christian. Are you certain of resurrection life? Why?

4. Which of the "ways of this world" did you follow before you knew Christ and that may even now be driving you? (See "The Ways of This World: A Flesh Inventory" on page 22 for suggestions.) Choose one or two and explain.

5. What did the "ways of this world" that you identified in Question 4 seem to promise you if you followed them?

When you made choices consistent with those "ways," were you ever satisfied? Did the drive or need go away? Explain.

6. Why do you think you are still tempted to follow these "ways of the world"?

7. In verses 5–6, Paul says that Christians have been "made alive" and are now seated with Christ. What practical difference does it make for you to know this, especially in relation to these ungodly drives or thoughts?

8. In verses 4–8, Paul concludes it is by grace that Christians are seated with Christ ("saved") and, by implication, are now able to deal with "the ways of the world."

Personalize verses 4–5: "Even though I was dead in my transgressions and sins, and I was driven _____(to get attention, to get approval, to get sexual satisfaction, to have my own way, to be better than, by rejection, by self-hate, by fear, by anxiety, or other), God _____." (Describe what God did for you and why.)

How might a heart revelation of what God did for you empower you to resist the lies and drives of the flesh?

9. Form your own definition for grace as you understand it from this passage.

The Truth About You

from Ephesians 1:3–14

I am blessed with what I need to overcome the flesh (v. 3).

My way to holiness and blamelessness before God is through Jesus (v. 4).

God wanted and was pleased to adopt me (v 5).

God freely gives his love to me. I do not have to do anything to earn it (v. 6).

God does not hold my sin against me because Jesus paid my penalty for me (v. 7).

God's Spirit is in me assuring me of who I am "in Christ" (vv. 13–14).

10. Grace does not mean that Christians are passive while God does all the work, but we are to actively respond with faith (v. 8). What exactly are we to have faith about? (See the sidebar, "The Truth About You.")

11. In verses 8–10, Paul mentions two kinds of "works." Explain the difference between the two.

12. What is the relationship between grace and good works in your life?

13. Identify one way you need to be strengthened by grace in this season of your life. (What do you need faith for in order to believe?)

RESPONDING TO GOD

Invite the Holy Spirit to increase your faith, especially in the areas for which you need to be strengthened. (You might find it helpful to talk and pray further with a trusted friend.)

GOD'S GRACE: POWER TO OVERCOME THE FLESH.

taking it further

Suggestions for application

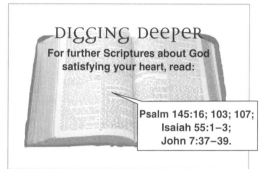

DIGGING DEEPER

For further Scriptures about God satisfying your heart, read:

Psalm 145:16; 103; 107;
Isaiah 55:1–3;
John 7:37–39.

Personal Expression

After reflecting on the grace of God at work in your life as you identified it in Question 4, think of a song that expresses your heart response to this truth. This week, listen to the song, read the words, or sing it.

Connecting to Life

Using the chart "The Ways of This World: A Flesh Inventory" on page 22, circle the primary attitudes at work in your everyday life. Then identify how these attitudes play out in situations and relationships. (See the examples below the chart.) Begin combating these lies with the truth you have learned in this study.

Meditation

Think through the implications of the truths in "The Truth About You" (page 18). An example:

Truth: I am blessed with what I need to overcome the flesh (Ephesians 1:3).

Implication: I do not need to feel hopeless, but I can ask God to show me how to move forward.

The Ways of This World: A Flesh Inventory

Sometimes the flesh that drives us toward sinful behavior can be rooted in wrong attitudes or conclusions we have drawn about God, ourselves, or life in general. Below is a list of such attitudes and feelings, although there are others also. Most of us experience any or all of these at some point in our lives, but the aim here is to focus on the main attitudes or feelings you recognize in yourself. Check the appropriate boxes:

❏ I am jealous	❏ I feel hopeless	❏ I must be right
❏ I am envious	❏ I feel isolated	❏ I cannot fail
❏ I am judgmental	❏ I must be better than . . .	❏ I must measure up to . . .
❏ I am critical	❏ I am no good	❏ I must have a great body
❏ I am bitter	❏ I feel lonely	❏ I must have a boy/girlfriend
❏ I am fearful	❏ I feel insecure	❏ I must seduce . . .
❏ I am self-righteous	❏ I feel inadequate	❏ I must be in control
❏ I am angry	❏ I must be perfect	❏ I am more spiritual than . . .
❏ I am never wrong	❏ I am good for nothing	❏ I feel dirty
❏ I am bad	❏ I am unlovable	❏ I am untouchable
❏ I am stained	❏ I don't fit in	❏ I don't need anyone
❏ I must be strong	❏ I'll do it myself	❏ I want more . . .
❏ I'll never get hurt again	❏ I'm an embarrassment	❏ No one is going to tell me what to do

These attitudes and feelings can lead to sinful behavior. Some examples are:

Attitude: "I must be better than . . ."

Result: Can lead to sins of jealousy, pride, tearing someone down in order to make yourself look better, or anger when someone else wins.

Attitude: "I am good for nothing."

Result: Can lead to sins of laziness, lack of taking appropriate responsibility, or a resistance to making a positive contribution to others. It can even lead to patterns of perfectionism in an effort to prove that the belief is not true.

Feeling: "I feel isolated."

Result: People who feel isolated often think God is distant and not available and so they do not draw on his presence and power in everyday circumstances. This makes them vulnerable to various temptations.

Realizing His Power
Ezekiel 36:22–27

Cathy knew what was expected of her: she needed to be more forgiving of people. She knew that's what the Bible says. And presumably that's what God's Spirit would say to her heart if she chose to listen. However, she couldn't stand people letting her down. She kept score. She paid people back. It was no wonder that her colleagues avoided her and her "demanding God." Unfortunately, she was the only Christian most of them knew.

We are all too much like Cathy. And surely God's plan to make himself known to others through people like us seems like a mistake. The prophet Ezekiel must have had the same thought as he lived among the sinful people of Israel. At times he was ready to give up on them. But God wasn't! God knew their limitations and he was at work to fulfill his promise and to complete his plan to redeem them. The solution? He, by his Spirit, would actually indwell his people so that he could teach them as well as empower them to demonstrate his character to others.

> **Live such good lives . . . that . . . they may see your good deeds and glorify God.**
>
> **—1 Peter 2:12**

Christians are the recipients of that promise. If only Cathy had listened to God. Surely his Spirit was stirring in her heart to reach out through her with his compassion and love.

How about you? What kind of God do you demonstrate to the people around you? Are you listening to God's Spirit in your heart? Are you reaching out for his power to respond to people the way he wants you to? Ask the Holy Spirit to open your eyes to this promise at work in you.

- What conclusions would your family and friends draw about God by watching your interactions with people?

- How has the responsiveness of your heart to God's voice changed in recent years?

- Finish this sentence: "My battle with sin is like . . ." (Examples: an insect fighting a monster, an equipped warrior disarming the enemy.)

enĝaĝinĝ the text

---

settinĝ the staĝe

- God made himself and his ways known to the nation Israel so that they could make him known to the rest of the nations.

- God expected Israel to live in a way consistent with his character (reflected in the Law he gave them) and thus demonstrate to the nations what he is like (the way Jesus shows us what the Father is like).

- Israel repeatedly failed in its mandate to make God known among the nations.

- Ezekiel is one of many prophets to confront the people of Israel with their failure.

- God promises Israel that he will do something to radically change an individual's ability to live consistently with God's character.

- Idols in the Old Testament usually consist of altars with statues of something other than the one true God. People obey the idol's demands even if it is in conflict with God's demands (for example, child sacrifice to satisfy the god Molech, see Leviticus 20:1–5).

- Idols can also be set up in a person's heart. An idol is anything a person obeys that opposes God or his ways. (This is in fact a way of seeking approval from something or someone other than God.)

Read Ezekiel 36:22–27

1. Explain in your own words what God says in verses 22–23. Be sure to identify any indications of how God might feel about this situation.

   What specific qualities of God's character do you see reflected in these verses?

2. What are the implications of Israel's failure (see Setting the Stage)?

3. Why do you think God has chosen to reveal himself (that is, his character) to the nations through his people?

4. Given that this passage refers to what God will do under the new covenant through Christians, how do you feel about your responsibility to reflect God's character to the people around you? Choose one and explain why:

- Overwhelmed
- Angry
- Privileged
- Crippled
- Natural
- Other:

5. The sin ("impurities") and idolatry of the Israelites are distorting God's character before the nations. Compare the idols of the Old Testament world with idols of today. (Refer to Setting the Stage and the results of Session One for help.)

6. There is a vast difference between the two hearts mentioned in verse 26. How would you describe the present condition of your own heart?

7. Identify a specific idol in your life. (See the article "Exposing Our Dark Secrets" for helpful suggestions.)

8. God makes a promise to deal effectively with sins and idols in the hearts of his people. Explain how this promise is real to you personally and at work in your life now.

Exposing Our Dark Secrets

Idolatry today is much more subtle and self-deceptive than in Ezekiel's time. Our "god" can be a friend, our self-image, our home, or even our work for God. Whenever we consistently obey a need instead of God's Spirit, we create an idol.

Because we depend so often on our idols for security and comfort, our hearts don't easily give them up. Emotions like fear, envy, jealousy, and the like are often indicators that an idol in our heart is being threatened.

In a speech, author Gordon MacDonald offered these questions to help us identify personal idols: Who am I trying to please? What needs am I trying to meet? What insecurities do I pamper? What rewards am I seeking? What fears am I fleeing? With whom do I compete? What guilt am I covering? When is there enough?

The Holy Spirit is eager to expose and free us from idolatry and self-deception. We simply need to be willing. Invite the Holy Spirit to expose any idols in your heart as you honestly answer the questions posed above. Don't be afraid. He wants to set you free!

9. Describe in your own words what verse 27 says God has done for you to enable you to live a godly life. (For a parallel Scripture verse, see Hebrews 8:10.)

10. God is at work in us to reflect his character in our lives. On a scale of 1 to 10, how consistently do you express his character in everyday circumstances? (1 = highly inconsistent; 10 = highly consistent.) Explain why you still struggle to do so.

1   2   3   4   5   6   7   8   9   10

11. In Titus 2:11–12, Paul says, "For the grace of God . . . teaches us to say 'No' to ungodliness and worldly passions, and to live self-controlled, upright and godly lives in this present age." Some have defined grace as God's willingness to forgive our sin. In light of Titus 2:11–12, is this definition sufficient? Explain.

Grace to Say No

Grace truly is amazing. This precious gift of God covers our sin and releases in us the resurrection power of Jesus. Yet despite its significance, some Christian leaders are reluctant to talk much about grace. They think that if people become aware of God's willingness to forgive sin, it will encourage them to keep on sinning. Instead, they preach a "get your act together or else" kind of message.

The apostle Paul strongly disagreed with this thinking. He taught that the way to stop sinning is to get an accurate understanding of the work of grace in us. Grace is that dynamic of God that moved him to express his unconditional love to us, even to the point of taking our sin upon himself (see 2 Corinthians 5:21) and enduring death for us (see Philippians 2:5–8). Our faith activates his grace in us, breaking the power of sin.

As we embrace the truth of who Jesus is and what he has done for us, we are empowered to say "no" to anything that would grieve him and "yes" to all that pleases him. Jesus said, "You will know the truth, and the truth will set you free" (John 8:32). The truth of grace produces freedom. And the truth is, we can't get enough of his amazing grace!

How would a better understanding of grace keep you from sinning?

12. How does God's grace make it possible for you to live a life that reflects his glory?

13. What steps can you take to cooperate more fully with God's grace at work in your life?

RESPONDING TO GOD

Ask the Holy Spirit to give you a responsive heart to his grace which is at work in you. Ask him to help you carry out the steps you have mentioned in Question 13.

GRACE RELEASES TRUTH AND POWER WITHIN US SO THAT WE CAN CHOOSE TO DO HIS WILL.

takinç it furtHer
Suggestions for application

DIÇÇINÇ DeepeR

For further study on God's provision for godly living see:

1 Corinthians 15:9–10;
Philippians 2:12–13;
Colossians 1:9–14;
2 Thessalonians 1:11;
2 Timothy 1:7;
1 Peter 1:3.

WORLD FOCUS

God's heart is that all nations would come to know him. Read the People Profile about the Kurds on the next two pages. Using the "Principles for Effective Intercession" (pages 104–5), pray for the Kurdish people.

Connecting to Life

Read the article "Grace to Say No" on page 30 and respond to the question: "How would a better understanding of grace keep you from sinning?"

Personal Expression

Find a stone that can represent your heart. Write on it the idol to which you are most susceptible. Keep this stone in a place where you will see it often throughout the course of this study on God's grace. Be in dialogue with the Holy Spirit about the idol.

PEOPLE PROFILE

the kurds—a Legacy of bitterness and bloodshed

Location: Turkey, Syria, Iraq, Iran. Population: 25.5 million. Religion: 99% Muslim.

"Ayad, look over by the well. It's that old fox Remzi," Massoud called. Ayad joined Massoud in his amazement. Both lads knew that Remzi wasn't welcome in the village. "This can only mean trouble," whispered Ayad. To the young boys it was inconceivable that Remzi would dare to enter the village unarmed while the family feud still raged.

The village streets were full of activity and music; Newroz (New Year) festivities were in full swing. Kurdish people were celebrating the passing of darkness (winter) and the arrival of light (spring). Houses were decorated with willow and quince branches, the new buds bringing life to the gray stone facades. Ayad and Massoud did not recognize many of the faces. Visitors and kinsmen from the surrounding valleys had flooded in for the Newroz celebrations.

Ayad spotted his father in the crowd, but before he could warn him of the trouble looming, he was stunned to see his father greet Remzi. Ayad's uncle caught Ayad by the arm, "It's all right, Ayad. It's Newroz! For now old feuds are put away. There will be plenty of time to settle old scores after the celebrations are over."

Living in a Christless world, the Kurds are an oppressed people caught in a cycle of unforgiveness and revenge. Genuine and lasting reconciliation of man to man and man to God can only come through Jesus Christ, God's Son (read Ephesians 2:12–16).

Pray that:
- The Kurdish people would come to know the One who made true reconciliation possible—Jesus Christ.
- God would protect this generation of children from growing up and inheriting the cycle of revenge and feuding that has plagued the Kurdish communities.
- During Newroz, the Kurdish festival celebrating the new year and the rebirth of light, the Holy Spirit would reveal the One who is the light of men (John 1:9).

GRASPING HIS LOVE
Isaiah 53:1–9

The lamb's scream stopped abruptly. The small Turkish boy watched, helpless, as his father slaughtered the little animal. He knew it had to be done, for once again the time had come for Muslim peoples everywhere to acknowledge their sin before God. His father dipped his finger in the lamb's blood and read a prayer of repentance. The lesson was only too obvious for the boy. Up until this point the lamb had been the boy's beloved pet, but now it had become a sacrifice for sin. He knew that sin must be paid for. But for him the price was painfully high.

Sin is costly. God paid an extremely high price to free us from it. His justice required the penalty of death for it (Romans 6:23). Jesus willingly chose to suffer that price, his love for each of us moving him to do so. By the life, death, and resurrection of Jesus, the power of sin has been broken and the debt of sin has been paid. Believing this foundational truth frees us from shame and empowers us to say "no" to that which grieves God's heart.

Jesus Christ ... gave himself for our sins to rescue us.

—GALATIANS 1:3—4

The cross where Jesus paid the price is a multifaceted symbol. It speaks of supreme love, costly sacrifice, deadly sin, assured forgiveness, the destruction of evil, the hope of freedom, and so much more.

What does the cross mean to you? As you go through this study, ask the Holy Spirit to open your eyes to a deeper understanding and application of the cross in your life.

PREPARING HEART AND MIND

- Brainstorm a list of words that comes to your mind when you think of the word *crucify*.

- Finish the following sentence: "Jesus loves me this I know [or "don't know"] because . . ."

- Identify someone in your life whom you are certain loves you and explain how you know that the person's love for you is real.

enɡaɡinɡ the text

settinɡ the staɡe

- Sin is anything which is not of God or according to his ways. God does not tolerate sin.

- The evil of sin must be acknowledged and paid for to satisfy God's justice. He cannot simply overlook it.

- God freely chose to pay the penalty for sin himself.

- Jesus set aside his rights as God and chose to come to earth in the form of a man (see Philippians 2:3–7). He lived without sinning. Since he was perfect and did not have to die to pay for his own sin, he could offer himself to die to pay for the sin of all individuals who put their faith in him.

- Through his death on the cross Jesus not only paid for our sins but broke the power of sin.

- Isaiah is a prophet living 700 years before Jesus is born. In chapter 53 he predicts the facts around Jesus' death and the reasons for it.

Read Isaiah 53:1–9

1. In one- to three-word statements, describe how Jesus is portrayed in verses 1–3.

2. Verses 4–6 contain many elements of the human experience and condition. Name them. (See "our" or "we" in the text.)

Which of these elements did Jesus identify with?

What did he do for us?

3. Considering your own human condition, what is one way in which Jesus identified with it that you most appreciate? Explain.

4. Jesus gave up his right as God and took the form of a bondservant (see Setting the Stage). Consider what Jesus let go of as well as what he embraced (took on) for your sake.

No More Shame

Ishmael eagerly awaited the birth. The Afghan villager already had three sons, and when a fourth was born, he and his wife rejoiced. Then Ishmael made a painful choice. He loved his new son, but he gave him to a neighbor who had no sons. In Afghan culture, only male children carry on the family identity. Shame covered every man who had no male offspring. Ishmael's gift lifted the shame from his neighbor's home.

A father giving away a beloved son is beyond our understanding. Yet that is precisely what God did for us. We were full of sin and shame. Nothing we did could change it. Motivated by his love for us, God gave away his one and only Son to set us free from the bondage of our shame.

Shame is a powerful force within us. It is not an emotion but a mind-set, a way of viewing ourselves. Healthy, well-balanced people feel guilt for something wrong they have *done*. Unhealthy people feel ashamed of who they *are*. Freedom from shame takes time, but it is possible. God has made a way through his beloved Son, Jesus.

Do you think and feel like a person who is deeply loved and treasured by someone significant? Why or why not?

5. What is it about God and sin that required Jesus to die on the cross? (See Setting the Stage.)

    Lord, help me to hate sin the way you do.

6. How do you think people's attitude toward sin today differs from the Bible's perspective?

7. How might a clearer understanding of what sin cost God strengthen you from sinning casually?

8. Romans 5:8 tells us: "But God demonstrates his own love for us in this: While we were still sinners, Christ died for us."

Explain how Isaiah 53:6–9 and Romans 5:8 illustrate God's love to you.

On a scale of 1 to 10 how convinced are you of God's love for you? (1 = unconvinced; 10 = highly convinced.) Explain.

1   2   3   4   5   6   7   8   9   10

9. How might a clearer understanding of God's extreme love for you strengthen you to resist sinning?

Love Beyond Understanding

A man who had worked in a Nazi concentration camp suffered a slow and painful death from disease. During his final days, memories of those he had tortured flooded his mind. Day and night he was haunted.

On the eve of his death, he called a Polish doctor to his side and confessed his evil, in hopes that this man would extend forgiveness on behalf of his people. The dying man waited, desperate to hear healing words. But the doctor never spoke. Words were not appropriate. He believed that this man deserved to die in agony for what he had done. Anything less would have minimized the pain of those who had died such cruel deaths.

We are all like this sinful man. We all deserve death, not forgiveness. Thankfully, God does not give us what we deserve. He didn't even wait till we stopped sinning, but while we were still in rebellion, hurting him and others, he died for us!

Consider this: God loves you for who you are, not for what you do.

10. In Romans 6:6–7, Paul says that Jesus died on the cross and that by faith "our old self was crucified with him so that the body of sin might be done away with, that we should no longer be slaves to sin — because anyone who has died has been freed from sin." How does one crucify the flesh by faith? (See "The Way to Freedom" on page 45 for help.)

11. What motive, drive, need, or impulse do you need to crucify? (It may help to think back to some of your answers in Sessions One and Two.)

The Way to Freedom

There is only one solution to deal effectively with the "flesh" and that is to kill (crucify) it. All Christians are expected not only to believe in Christ's death for them (1 Timothy 1:15–16) but also to be crucified with him (Galatians 2:20). Jesus indicated this when he told his disciples to take up their cross and follow him.

However, taking up the Lord's cross is not always what we think it might be. In the story of the two sisters, Mary and Martha, in Luke 10:38–42, Martha believed that cooking was her cross to bear. On the other hand, she thought Mary had not yet learned to deny herself—that she was doing the easy thing by listening to Jesus.

Like many of us today, Martha misunderstood Jesus. Picking up our cross is not necessarily an unpleasant expectation for us. The cross is the process and the place that keeps us completely dependent on God. It is where we refuse to do anything for any other reason than to please Jesus.

If Mary had a need to please her sister, she did not respond to it. If the only way she felt comfortable around Jesus was to be working for him, she died to that too. If she felt self-conscious doing what only those of the male gender did in her culture, she also brought that concern to the cross. She just sat and listened, taking in Jesus' truth like a rapt scholar. Mary's cross was to say "no" to anything that would have led her away from Jesus.

The cross gives us the power to say "no" to lies, sinful attitudes and patterns of behavior, and fears about what others think, and to say "yes" to Jesus.

What do you have to "die" to in order to yield completely to Jesus?

Take time to thank God for the cross. Invite him to lead you to crucify the specific "flesh" you identified in Question 11.

the cross:
the only doorway
to freedom.

taking it further

Suggestions for application

DIGGING DEEPER

For further study on Jesus and the cross see:

Galatians 3:10–13;
Philippians 2:6–8;
Colossians 1:19–20;
1 Timothy 2:3–6;
Hebrews 4:14–16;
10:5–9.

Personal Expression

Find or make a small wooden cross. (You could simply attach two pencils or sticks together.) Take time to think about what Jesus did for you on the cross to free you from sin, and why he did it. Write your answer to Question 11 on a piece of paper and fix it to that cross. Invite the Holy Spirit to empower you to say "no" to that motive, drive, need, or impulse. Put it in a place where you will see it for the duration of this Bible study.

Connecting to Life

Read "Love Beyond Understanding" on page 43, then respond to the statement: "Consider this: God loves you for who you are, not what you do."

Meditation

The cross of Jesus speaks of supreme love, costly sacrifice, deadly sin, assured forgiveness, the destruction of evil, the hope of freedom, and so much more. Take some time to reflect on the meaning of the cross. Write in your own words what it symbolizes to you.

Recognizing the traps
2 Samuel 11:1–12:24

Toby never dreamed he would fall in love with another man's wife, let alone the wife of his Christian friend, Kevin. Then again, few people ever intend to break up someone else's marriage. But now Toby was obsessed with thoughts of Jan, his friend's wife. He lived for the moments he spent in her presence: the Sunday morning service, midweek gatherings, the occasional social event. He even joined the same home group to be around her more. Almost without thinking, he increased his phone contact with Kevin and often dropped by their home to watch the game of the week, or simply to chat. Nothing looked wrong on the outside. But regardless of the pretense, Toby had only one thing in mind, and he was almost ready to make his move. He had enough indications from Jan to guess that she was interested.

Search me, O God, and know my heart.

— psalm 139:23

The power of sin is continually present to ensnare Christians whenever possible. Satan is well aware that our hearts are not always set on God and his truth. He knows the perfect line to get our attention and does all he can to keep us focused on the object of our potential downfall. He has mastered the skill through the centuries. In 2 Samuel 11 and 12, King David discovers this fact. In spite of his heart for God, David chooses to destroy a marriage and a human life simply to satisfy his flesh.

Mercifully for Toby, his obsession had been noticed. One of his friends intervened by lovingly confronting him with his concerns. Shocked by the truth of what his friend had observed, Toby knew he had to take radical action to escape the trap of his obsession. Temptation does not have to lead to sin. There is a way out. God is actively working in the Christian heart to remind us that we are set apart and indwelt by his holy presence. He will stir the hearts of Christian friends to help us stay on track—God's track.

Are you sensitive to the Holy Spirit's voice in the midst of temptation? Ask God to open your eyes to see the traps before you are ensnared, or if necessary, to empower you to escape.

PREPARING HEART AND MIND

- What is the worst part of being in a cycle of sin and deception?

- What role do your friends play in strengthening you to say "no" to sin?

- In what way is your prayer life impacting your ability to hear and obey God at present?

encacinc the text

setting the stage

- Old Testament worship is based on the truth that God is holy, sin is evil, and sin separates people from their holy God.

- Even in Old Testament days, God's grace is available for sin. The priesthood, the temple, and the various sacrifices are all given to the Jews as a means of grace—that is, as a way to deal with sin so that God can be in their midst.

- The Old Testament means of grace are validated as true by the life, death, and resurrection of Jesus.

- David understands that God requires people to take responsibility for their sin (admit to it) and to repent of it (turn from it) in order to receive God's forgiveness.

- Uriah, a Hittite who has converted to faith in Israel's God, is one of David's trusted "mighty men" (2 Samuel 23:8, 39). Bathsheba's grandfather is David's most trusted adviser (2 Samuel 23:34; 15:12).

Read 2 Samuel 11:1–12:24

1. From chapter 11, describe the kind of man Uriah appears to be from his behavior.

2. Identify the ways David sins against Uriah and God in chapter 11 (see also Setting the Stage):

   v. 1

   vv. 2–3

vv. 4–5

vv. 6–7

v. 13

vv. 14–15

v. 25

Which of these sins is the most shocking to you?

3. David makes several wrong choices. Consider what actions he could have taken to avoid each sin and how easy or difficult it would have been for him to do so.

4. Why do you think people who love God get into such messes?

Facing Our Own Sin

The cover-up grew more and more complicated as David tried to hide one sin with another. We too can be trapped in a web of deceit spun by our own sinful choices. Even when our sin is obvious to everyone else, we may still refuse to acknowledge it. In his love for David, God would not allow him to continue living as if all was well when in reality it wasn't. Through his prophet Nathan he helped David see the painful consequences of his actions. Just as God pursued David to confront him with his sin, so God also pursues us. He wants us to be set free from the bondage and power of sin.

Breaking out of denial, facing the harm that has been done, and asking God and others for forgiveness are our steps to freedom. God's forgiveness is certain. The question is: Will we acknowledge that we need it? Will we, like David, respond in repentance when confronted by the truth? *How can you be sure you are not walking in denial by refusing to face your sin?*

5. God helps David face the reality of his sin through the wise confrontation of Nathan. In what ways have friends played a similar role as Nathan in your life?

What kinds of things can you do to invite people to speak into your life?

6. In the introduction story, Toby's friend "lovingly confronted" him. When attempting to confront someone with your concerns, what is important to consider, both in *what* you say and *how* you say it?

7. David's response to Nathan and God is admirable (12:13). What do you think David believes about God and about himself, for him to make such a response?

    How do your views of God and yourself compare with David's?

8. Hebrews 4:16 invites us to "approach the throne of grace with confidence, so that we may receive mercy and find grace to help us in our time of need." A "time of need" may be in the midst of the temptation as well as after we have chosen to sin. Is it easier for you to talk to God while you are in the midst of a temptation (such as when David is scheming Uriah's death), or after you sin and you are in need of forgiveness? Explain.

    What would keep you from approaching this throne of grace?

9. Although God forgives David, there are consequences to his sin (12:13–23). What are those consequences, and why do you think God allows David to experience them?

Altar of Reconciliation

Chris had never felt so wretched. His latest girlfriend had left him, saying she'd had enough of his partying and drinking. He'd suddenly seen how selfishly he lived. But how could he start afresh? He had nothing to offer God to "make up" for his selfishness. Then it hit him. What he'd heard in church as a child was true: *Jesus paid the price for his sin!* Empty-handed, yet with faith welling up in his heart, Chris repented, turned from his selfishness, and discovered a whole new relationship with God.

God designed the tabernacle and its worship (described in the Old Testament in Exodus, Leviticus, Numbers, and Deuteronomy) for a specific purpose—to teach the Israelites that he wanted a relationship with them. The sin that separated them from him could be dealt with at the altar. Once the sin was repented of and paid for by blood sacrifice, God and the offenders were reconciled.

When we received Jesus Christ as our Savior, we also came to this altar. Like Chris, we repented, believing that Jesus' blood paid for our sins and that his death broke the power of sin in us. Then we received his gift of life.

For us as Christians, this altar remains a key to freedom and intimacy with Jesus. Anytime we recognize sin we can freely approach God, repent, and receive forgiveness. The blood of Jesus is always available to wash us clean and restore fellowship with him.

Picture yourself approaching God with sin. Does that picture reflect biblical truth?

10. Identify the many ways God's grace is demonstrated to David in this story.

11. If you are trapped in a cycle of sin and condemnation (no matter how minor), how can God's grace help you?

RESPONDING TO GOD

Take time to wait in silence before responding in prayer. Express to God what is stirring in your heart.

GOD OPPOSES THE PROUD BUT GIVES GRACE TO THE HUMBLE.

1 Peter 5:5

taking it further

Suggestions for application

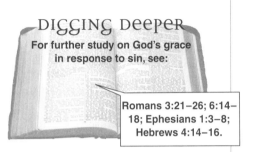

DIGGING DEEPER

For further study on God's grace in response to sin, see:

Romans 3:21–26; 6:14–18; Ephesians 1:3–8; Hebrews 4:14–16.

Connecting to Life

Read through the article "Facing Our Own Sin" on page 52. Respond to the question: "How can you be sure you are not walking in denial by refusing to face your sin?"

Meditation

Take time to think through Psalm 139 with the following in mind:

1. Identify all words describing God or his activity.
2. Personalize all phrases that describe God's interaction with people.
3. Now write out some reasons why you can confidently invite God into your struggle with temptation and sin.

Personal Expression

Write a poem or song that expresses your heart's response to God's great grace.

Responding in Grace
2 Corinthians 11:1–12:10

Mark had not slept soundly in months. He was keenly aware that his wife's side of the bed was empty. Images of the accident still haunted him: the screech of the brake, the crash, the blood everywhere. Her death had been instantaneous, but somehow he had walked away from the accident with only minor injuries.

Mark was tormented with bitterness. He was angry that God had allowed his wife to be taken away, and he resisted even the thought of forgiving the drunk who killed her. Never had he anticipated anything like this ever happening to him.

But life is full of difficult moments. People sin. Sickness hits. Babies die. Spouses fail. Friends betray. Having faith in Jesus does not eliminate hardship from a Christian's life. The apostle Paul certainly knows this to be true. In fact, Paul's life as a Christian is full of challenges, including a "thorn in the flesh" which he says tormented him. Unlike Mark, Paul does not allow his heart to harden. He continues to reach out in love,

Do not repay anyone evil for evil.

—ROMANS 12:17

as well as to face hardship with remarkable courage and strength. Things he cannot change he embraces, knowing that God's grace is sufficient.

How about you? Are you demanding more out of life than what you have? Is it possible that you are holding on to an offense that is poisoning your heart? Ask the Holy Spirit to show you where your heart needs to be strengthened by grace.

- How do you usually respond when someone close hurts you?

- What are some unmet expectations that influence your heart and attitudes?

- Finish the sentence: "When I think of the future I feel . . ." Explain your answer.

eNGaGiNG tHe text

Read 2 Corinthians 11:1–12:10

<table>
<tr><td>

setting tHe stage

- The Corinthian believers come primarily from a pagan background.

- Paul is their main spiritual father and leader, having lived among them for eighteen months. He also visits them and writes to them several times.

- False teachers, most likely from Jewish backgrounds, have challenged Paul's apostolic authority by attacking his motives as well as his understanding of the gospel.

- Forgiveness is a choice a person makes to not hold something against someone else. Forgiveness is not necessarily felt, although one may pass through a wide range of feelings in the process of forgiving the other person.

</td><td>

1. What do we learn about the origin and early dynamics of Paul's relationship with the Corinthians? (See Setting the Stage for help.)

2. What seems to be the present problem in their relationship?

3. Identify specific actions or attitudes of the Corinthians that might have offended Paul. Explain. (See also Setting the Stage.)

</td></tr>
</table>

4. If you were Paul, how do you think you might have responded to the Corinthians?

5. Consider Paul's heart attitude toward the Corinthians in light of the present troubles. Choose from the words below what best describes his attitude and explain why.

- hard
- hurt
- persistently loving
- angry
- compassionate
- other:

6. How do you usually respond when someone sins against you?

7. We can learn from Paul's response to the Corinthians. Identify some of the elements of his response that you could apply when you are tempted to take offense.

Letting Go of the Past

Hurt caused by family members, especially in our youth, has a profound impact on us. How we respond to the pain has huge implications for our emotional and spiritual health.

God knows about our pain and wants to lead us to hope and to wholeness. We should first acknowledge to him and to a trusted friend what has happened and how it has affected us. If we still live in an abusive situation, immediate help may be necessary to protect ourselves. Whatever else must be done, we need to keep our hearts from hardening. The Lord wants to assist us in forgiving those who have hurt us. He knows we'll be tempted to indulge in bitterness, vengeance, or self-pity. But as we acknowledge our sinful reactions and receive his power to forgive, a new measure of Jesus' life is released in us.

Identify past offenses that are presently affecting you. Ask God to help you "let go" of the pain and extend forgiveness to the offender.

8. Paul lists a variety of experiences that he has lived through. If you had gone through these, which one would have most tempted you to harden your heart toward God and life in general? Explain.

9. How would God's grace keep a person's heart soft and responsive in the midst of circumstances like these that Paul lists?

10. In 12:1–6, Paul describes an experience he had just before Barnabas invited him to go to Antioch. What happened to Paul?

11. God allowed Paul to suffer from something Paul calls a "thorn in my flesh." Describe the process Paul went through with God that eventually enabled him to accept this thorn.

12. If we understand a "thorn" to be any unwanted circumstance in our lives, think of a "thorn" in your life. How might God's grace help you to deal practically with the situation?

Letting Go of the Future

If I can't do something about a problem, it's not a problem but a fact of life." Understanding this truth is a must for every leader, according to author John Maxwell.

The apostle Paul certainly understood this truth. He was a leader of leaders, who focused on his purpose, lived by his values, and walked in harmony with God. He determined to make an impact on the key cities of his world, and he did! His influence has since been multiplied in millions of lives through the centuries.

What was the key to his success? For one thing, he embraced the "thorn" in his life that couldn't be changed. He let go of his expectations of God, of himself, and of life—expectations that couldn't be fulfilled. He refused to be crippled by bitterness, pity, or self-defeat. He asked God to remove the thorn, but accepted God's answer. He recognized God's purpose in it. And he was satisfied by the reality of God's grace to help him live with it.

Whatever his "thorn," it was a constant reminder that he was simply a man through whom a great God chose to work. God's mighty grace to live victoriously is made real to us as we embrace the things we cannot change in our lives.

What problem in your life are you powerless to change? Have you released it to God?

RESPONDING to GOD

Invite the Holy Spirit to help you see what you might need to let go of (such as expectations of how things should be, rights you have, and so on).

Let go.
God knows what
He's doing.

taking it further

Suggestions for application

DIGGING DEEPER

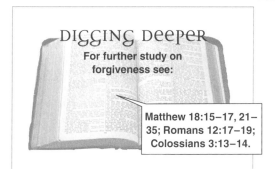

For further study on forgiveness see:

Matthew 18:15–17, 21–35; Romans 12:17–19; Colossians 3:13–14.

Personal Expression

Create a poster that depicts your heart shedding those things that tend to harden you. Write a caption for the picture that invites you to respond to God with the trust and love of a bride for her husband.

Connecting to Life

It is possible to hold on to rights or expectations in such a way that our hearts become hardened with discontent, resentment, or bitterness until we get what we want. Identify one or more demands or rights which you are holding on to. Invite the Holy Spirit to empower you to relinquish your rights and thus let go of that demand. (Some examples are: the right to be married, to have children, to have certain material things, to have good health, to be understood.)

WORLD FOCUS

Identify a situation in the world where a people or a nation face opposition of some sort. (Some recent examples: racial tensions, such as between the Serbs and Kosovar Albanians; political refugees, such as the Kurds; a nation under unjust rule, such as Afghanistan under the Taliban.) Pray for God's grace to strengthen these peoples to forgive those who have abused them.

fINISHING STRONG
Ephesians 6:10–18; Philippians 3:7–14

session
SIX

Joan wept uncontrollably. In the few months since coming to church, she had grown to appreciate and trust this caring couple, and now, as they prayed for her, the old pain surfaced. Their prayers were focused on words that had been spoken against her, cutting words that had pierced her heart and still enslaved her even after twenty years. At last the Holy Spirit was uprooting those old lies and working to renew her mind with the truth. In the weeks that followed, Joan grew in Christ, learning to drink in God's truth and thus protect her heart from any further deadly attacks.

Slander, gossip, and accusation are deadly weapons. Words are incredibly powerful when carefully crafted and spoken with the intention to cripple and destroy. The enemy himself is a master at it. He especially targets Christians as he attempts to keep them from bearing godly fruit. And, as the apostle Paul discovered, even fellow Christians can be the ones to speak out the enemy's fatal lies. Christians from Jerusalem tried to bring down both him and his ministry with their words.

"No weapon forged against you will prevail."

—ISAIAH 54:17

But Paul still finishes strong. He keeps his eye fixed on his main goal in life: to worship God and live for his glory. Paul's life bears fruit in every kind of situation, even in prison in Rome. He chooses not to react to people who intend to hurt him, responding to them in a different spirit. How does he do it? He has learned to press on, listening to the Spirit "on all occasions" (Ephesians 6:18), and through the Spirit he continually wears "the full armor of God" (Ephesians 6:11).

How about you? Are you drawing from the ministry of the Spirit within to keep you strong, even when weapons are aimed to put you down? Are you pressing on toward an eternal goal? Invite the Holy Spirit to help you see all that he has provided so that you will finish strong.

PREPARING HEART AND MIND

- Finish the following sentence: "I lose spiritual strength when I . . ." Explain.

- What is the difference between protecting your heart in a healthy way and an unhealthy hardening of your heart?

- Given what the people around you see, hear, and experience when they are with you, what would they say your ultimate purpose in life is?

enᴄaᴄinᴄ tнe text

setinᴄ тнe staᴄe

- A Roman soldier's back is unprotected and thus vulnerable to the enemy's attack. The soldiers fight in such a way that the group is responsible for protecting one another's backs, rather than each soldier defending himself.

- Of all the pieces of armor, the belt is the essential piece that holds other parts in their proper place.

- In the letter to the Ephesians, Paul has already laid the foundation that Christians are *seated* with Christ and have resurrection power to *walk* out their faith. He now continues by encouraging them to *stand* strong in the authority they have "in Christ."

Read Ephesians 6:10–18

1. When Paul writes: "Be strong in the Lord and in his mighty power," what do you think he means (v. 10)? (See Setting the Stage.)

2. Explain in your own words how you draw upon the Lord's "mighty power."

3. People do cooperate with Satan (usually unknowingly) and they do sin against us. How might Paul's reminder that our battle is not against people but against Satan and his forces (v. 12) help you to respond appropriately?

4. Using the analogy of putting on Roman armor, Paul lists six basic elements that God has provided to strengthen believers, such as the helmet of salvation. Identify the five other pieces of Roman armor with their spiritual equivalent:

   1.
   2.
   3.
   4.
   5.

5. *The belt:* Why is truth so essential in a battle with Satan?

   How do you "put on" truth?

6. *The breastplate:* In Philippians 3:9 Paul tells us that righteousness is a gift, but here he tells us to put it on. How do you "put on" righteousness?

How does putting on righteousness strengthen us against Satan?

Seeing with new Eyes

Helen was struggling for her life. The water in the huge pool kept pulling her back, like an undertow at the shore. Meanwhile, those around her were indifferent to her cries. Some even hoped she would drown. As she lifted her head and gasped for breath, she saw Jesus, but she would not let him help her. She simply continued to swim on, determined to make it. Then she woke up!

This dream changed Helen's life. Through it God revealed that her view of life was distorted. He went on to free her with the truths that he is trustworthy, that he provides people who care, and that he gives her significance.

We all have a grid through which we perceive life, comprising conclusions we've drawn about ourselves, God, and life in general. These include falsehoods like "I'm worthless," "God expects perfection," or "It's impossible to live without sex." These perceptions strongly influence our actions. For example, if we think, "I must never fail," we'll either be driven to be perfect or refuse to try altogether.

The Holy Spirit actively works to transform our mental grids. When we demonstrate behavior or attitudes that are rooted in wrong thinking, he not only convicts us of the sin but works to expose the lie. All the while he is nurturing us with truth to set us free and help us more consistently respond like Jesus.

What picture do you have of yourself and God? Any distortions of the truth?

7. *The sandals:* The "gospel of peace" means it is a gospel that brings reconciliation between God and man and between one another. How does being ready to walk in reconciliation (with God and with others) undermine Satan?

8. *The shield:* Identify some of the flaming arrows Satan tends to throw at you. How can faith shield you from their destructive effect?

   How might your faith help to shield someone else? (See note about Roman soldiers in Setting the Stage.)

9. *The sword:* In what way is the Word of God like a sword? (See also Hebrews 4:12.)

How satisfied are you with your interaction with God through his Word?

10. Identify one step you can take to strengthen your armor and thus your stand as you face life's challenges. (An example: Consider a personal relationship that needs reconciliation. What can you do at this point to move toward reconciliation?)

Read Philippians 3:7–14

11. A personal mission statement answers the question: "What is my life ultimately about?" In these verses Paul basically answers that question. Put in your own words what you think Paul's mission statement would be. (Use about fifteen words.)

Seekers Will Find Him

Of all the things we could boast about—our intellect, wealth, good looks, power, or achievements—the only thing that carries weight with God is our relationship with him. The apostle Paul said that his highest goal was "that I may gain Christ" (Philippians 3:8). God is a God who wants to be known by us, and the wonderful thing is that every one of us can know him.

He declares in Proverbs 8:17, "I love those who love me, and those who seek me find me." Seeking God is the key to knowing him. And when we do seek him, we won't be disappointed. We will find a loving God of faultless character. We will know a God who delights in kindness, justice, and faithfulness.

To know him is to love and feed on his written Word, the Bible. To know him is to pursue him in friendship, as Moses did in the Tent of Meeting (see Exodus 33:7–11). And to know him is to worship him, as David did in the caves and courts of Israel (see Psalm 52; 65; 84).

What are you doing to get to know God? Pursue him as you would a treasured friend.

12. Identify some key words or phrases that begin to describe your life's purpose.

What role can God's grace play in you fulfilling your purpose?

Thank God for his grace-filled provision of spiritual armor that protects you against the enemy. Invite him to empower you daily to use it so that you can finish strong.

HE WILL KEEP YOU STRONG TO THE END.

1 Corinthians 1:8

taking it further

Suggestions for application

DIGGING DEEPER

For further study on our protection and refuge in God, see:

Psalm 11; 37:1–15; 57; 64; 71; Isaiah 54:11–17.

Personal Expression

Take the stone on which you wrote the name of an idol from the "Personal Expression" in Session Two. Think about what God has done throughout this session to set you free from idols. As an act of faith, stand in an open field or other large open area and throw the stone as far as you can. Thank God for your new heart!

Connecting to Life

In about fifteen words create your own personal mission statement that captures your reason or motives for living. Then think about your next ten years. (It may be helpful to identify key transitions like graduation, marriage or baby, job change, or retirement.) What can you do to insure your next ten years reflect your personal mission statement?

WORLD FOCUS

The Gond people are in need of the Lord and the armor he provides. Read about them on page 79 and pray for this people group of India to come to know him. "Principles for Effective Intercession" (pages 104–5) may also be helpful.

PEOPLE PROFILE

the gond—awaiting a new destiny

Location: India. Population: 7.3 million. Religion: 60% Hindu, 40% Animist.

Lachi's brow furrowed as she glanced at Malku's vain attempts to crawl. Almost all the village children had been delivered by Lachi. Malku's birth had seemed normal; all the birth rituals had been observed. The clan gods received proper offerings, and the water spirits were appeased. Yet Malku refused milk, put on little weight, and now, months later, hardly had the strength to crawl.

In the back of her mind, Lachi suppressed a troubled thought. A light was kept near every newborn Gond for the first twenty-four hours. The candle helped the gods to see the child and write his destiny. Sri Brahma used the light to prophesy the child's fate from his great book; Sri Satvi used the light to write the child's fate on his forehead; Hiras Guru gifted the newborn with the power of speech. But during Malku's first night, Lachi had dropped the candle, plunging the room into darkness.

Was her clumsiness that night the cause of Malku's problems? Were the gods angered by the sudden darkness? Did they prophesy illness and weakness over Malku in their anger? If only she could read the invisible prophecy on the child's brow. Lachi was haunted by the thought that she was responsible for the awful destiny the gods had prophesied over the child.

Neither Lachi nor her Gond people have ever heard the words of another prophecy—the words of God spoken through Jeremiah: "'I know the plans I have for you,' declares the LORD, 'plans to prosper you and not to harm you, plans to give you hope and a future'" (Jeremiah 29:11).

Pray that:

- The Gond would come to know the true God, who desires only good for men and women.
- Jeremiah 29:11 would be proclaimed over the Gond.
- The Gond would hear and believe the truth of Ephesians 1:4–6, that God has a special destiny for every Gond to be a member of God's own family.

Leader's Notes

L eading a Bible study—especially for the first time—can make you feel both nervous and excited. If you are nervous, realize that you are in good company. Many biblical leaders, such as Moses, Joshua, and the apostle Paul, felt nervous and inadequate to lead others (see, for example, 1 Corinthians 2:3). Yet God's grace was sufficient for them, just as it will be for you.

Some excitement is also natural. Your leadership is a gift to the others in the group. Keep in mind, however, that other group members also share responsibility for the group. Your role is simply to stimulate discussion by asking questions and encouraging people to respond. The suggestions below can help you to be an effective leader.

The Role of the Holy Spirit

Always remember that the work of the Holy Spirit is necessary in order for each of us to understand and apply God's Word. Prayer, your prayer for one another, is critical for revelation to take place. You can be assured that God is working in every group member's life. Look for what is stirring in people's hearts. Listen to their statements and questions, and be aware of what they do not say as well as what they do say. Watch God do his work. He will help you lead others and feed you at the same time. May God's blessing be with you.

Preparing to Lead

1. Ask God to help you understand and apply the passage to your own life. Unless this happens, you will not be prepared to lead others.

2. Carefully work through each question in the study guide. Meditate and reflect on the passage as you formulate your answers.
3. Familiarize yourself with the leader's notes for the session. These will help you understand the purpose of the session and will provide valuable information about the questions.
4. Pray for the various members of the group. Ask God to use these studies to help you grow as disciples of Jesus Christ.
5. Before each meeting, make sure each person has a study guide. Encourage them to prepare beforehand for each study.

Leading the Study

Opening (approximately 5 minutes)

1. At the beginning of your first time together, take a little extra time to explain that the Living Encounters are designed for discussions, sharing, and prayer together, not as lectures. Encourage everyone to participate, but realize that some may be hesitant to speak during the first few sessions.
2. Begin on time. If people realize that the study begins on schedule, they will work harder to arrive on time. Open in prayer. You may then want to ask for feedback from one person who has followed through on the "Taking It Further" section from the previous week's study.
3. Read the introduction together. This will orient the group to the passage being studied.

Preparing Heart and Mind (approximately 15 minutes)

1. Although these questions may be considered by individuals beforehand, you are strongly encouraged to begin your group time with them. They are designed to provoke thinking about a topic that is directly related to the study. Anyone who wrestles with one or more

of the questions will be better prepared to receive the truth found in the rest of the study.

2. If your time is very limited, encourage your group members to consider one or more of the questions before they arrive. It is not necessary to mention them in your meeting. However, you may want to ask for one person who has already considered the questions to share thoughts about one question with the group before moving on to "Engaging the Text."

Engaging the Text (approximately 50 minutes)

1. This section is a study of one or more passages of Scripture. Read the Scripture portion(s) aloud. You may choose to do this yourself, or you might ask for volunteers.

2. There are normally 10–12 questions, which will take the group through an inductive process of looking at the text. These questions are designed to be used just as they are written. If you wish, you may simply read each one aloud. Or you may prefer to express a question in your own words until it is clearly understood. Unnecessary rewording, however, is not recommended.

3. Don't be afraid of silence. People in the group may need time to think before responding.

4. Avoid answering your own questions. Even an eager group will quickly become passive and silent if they think the leader will do most of the talking.

5. Encourage more than one answer to each question. Ask, "What do the rest of you think?" or, "Anyone else?" until several people have had a chance to respond.

6. Try to be affirming whenever possible. Let people know you appreciate their insights into the passage.

7. Never reject an answer. If it is clearly wrong, ask, "Which verse led you to that conclusion?" Or let the group handle the problem by asking them what they think about the question.

8. Avoid going off on tangents. If people wander off course, gently bring them back to the passage being considered.
9. End on time. This will be easier if you control the pace of the discussion by not spending too much time on some questions or too little on others.

Articles

There are several articles in each study that are set off by gray boxes. These offer additional information as well as help to liven up the group time. "Setting the Stage" relates directly to the study of the passage, and questions will refer you to this sidebar when needed. Other gray-boxed articles can further illustrate or apply a principle. Become acquainted with the articles beforehand so that you know what is available. Remember that reading one or more of these articles in the group will add to your meeting time.

Responding to God (approximately 10 minutes)

In every study guide a prayer response is built into the last few minutes of the group time. This is to allow for the Holy Spirit to bring further revelation as well as application of the truths studied into each person's life. Usually there is a suggested way to respond in prayer, but feel free to adjust that as you sense what God is doing.

Taking It Further

You may want to encourage people to do one or more of these suggestions during the week ahead. Perhaps ask one person to share about it at your next time together. Or, depending on your time constraints, you may choose to do some of these activities during your session together.

Many more suggestions and helps are found in the book *Leading Bible Discussions* (InterVarsity Press). Reading it would be well worth your time.

Rising Above

Ephesians 2:1–10

Purpose: To confront the participants with the reality and nature of their "flesh," which competes with the Spirit of God in them, and to help them grasp the truth that God is at work within them to empower them to "put to death" their flesh.

Setting the Stage

This sidebar helps the participant to understand the circumstances and background of Paul's letter to the Ephesians.

Engaging the Text

Question 1 There is a fundamental difference between Christians and non-Christians. Christians are "alive," in a place of power, and are created "in Christ Jesus to do good works" (Ephesians 2:10). Non-Christians are without Christ and "dead," following Satan's ways and producing transgressions and sins.

Question 2 Like people today, the Ephesians were driven by such things as their desires, needs, and so on.

Question 3 Some things Paul was driven by were his desire to live up to the law and his need to earn God's favor. He worked hard to earn God's acceptance. But it is impossible for people to live up to God's standards on their own. Attempting to do so opens the door to pride in self, condemnation of others, self-righteousness, and so forth. When Paul reacted violently to the Christian's claim that the Messiah was for all peoples regardless of their background (Acts 7:1ff; 9:1ff), his reaction exposed his wrong thinking toward what makes people worthy of God. His wrong answer: their works. The right answer is that God created people in his image for relationship with him. God loves them. Being driven like Paul by pride, self-righteousness, or violent anger is just as sinful as being driven by greed or sexual passion.

Question 4 Some examples are: a need to earn God's approval; a need to satisfy your sexual drive; a need to be recognized; a need for more (greed); a need to measure up; a need to be in control; anxiety; fear. This is meant to be a quick exercise. One or two examples should jump out, as wrong motives are usually obvious to people. It is important to let participants choose to share as they feel safe to do so. Some may feel extremely vulnerable and not be used to talking about such personal things. Let them know that it is fine to be silent.

Question 5 Example of a choice: "Driven by a need for recognition, I consistently pushed my opinion until I was recognized. Was I satisfied? No. My real problem was insecurity. No momentary attention satisfied me. It simply whet my appetite for more." The answer to this question will vary and will not necessarily be logical, as the flesh is not always logical! This is part of the point of this exercise: for people to realize that they are being sucked in by lies concerning comfort, relief, lasting love, assurance of personal value, or any number of other things.

Question 6 The "why" behind people's sinful habits is sometimes very complex. Many times it is rooted in lies about self or God that were concluded from painful situations of our past. The ministry of the Holy Spirit within is critical to gain freedom. It is not enough to simply analyze ourselves. This question is simply trying to raise people's awareness that sinful patterns are actually not life-giving.

Question 7 Christians have been rescued from an existence without God and his power to live rightly. They are now with God "in Christ," in his place of authority. However, our flesh is often the loudest voice we hear, and for those addicted to a habit, it is the only voice they obey. Why? They are believing a lie: "I cannot live without this." Alternatively, they are masking a lie they do not want to face. The habit keeps them preoccupied so that they don't have to face, for example, a sense of shame ("I am bad"). There are endless examples.

This passage speaks of a relationship Christians now have with God himself. We are with him in his place and it is a place of *power.* Through the love and acceptance God gives us, we can be strengthened to hear and obey God's voice.

Question 8 The Holy Spirit within us continually reinforces the truth about God's character. He also speaks to us about God's commitment to us and his love for us. Thus he uproots with the truth the very lies that empower flesh.

Question 10 It is important that people realize their part. We are to believe the truth about God and his love for us. We are to believe God has indeed rescued us from darkness, forgiven us, adopted us, and that he offers his power to us on all occasions.

Question 11 The first "works" are what people do to try to earn salvation or God's approval. The second "works" are what people do because they *have* God's approval and are now empowered by him to do them.

Question 13 It is critical that people are aware not only of their flesh (most are very aware of it), but also that God is willing and able to interact with them in facing it. Sadly, people often feel so ashamed of their flesh that they don't talk to God about it, except to say, "I'm sorry. I'll try harder." Instead, we need to say to God, "I'm sorry. What can *we* do about this?" Encourage participants to invite God into their situation.

Responding to God It is important for people to take time to respond to the truths they have just been looking at. If participants are not used to praying in a large group, it may be appropriate to divide into twos or threes to pray together.

Taking It Further

While not a requirement, the aim of these suggestions is to help the study have a continuing effect on lives through the following week. Encourage people to choose one or more of the activities which appeal to them. Make it clear that they are not expected to follow through on all the suggestions.

ReaLizinɡ His Power

Ezekiel 36:22–27

Purpose: To remind participants that Christians have a mandate from God to show the world what he is like. God has made it possible for us to do that through the work of Jesus on the cross and the ministry of the Holy Spirit.

Engaging the Text

Question 1a The aim of this question is to help people recognize the situation from God's perspective. He has been faithfully revealing himself to the Jews, and he has been longing for the other nations to come to know him too, but the Jews are not faithfully representing him. In fact, they are giving the peoples around them such a bad impression of God that other nations are profaning him. God seems angry, and the reason for his anger is probably because he is longing for relationship with the peoples he created but is being prevented from this. God seems determined for people to know him, and he refuses to give up on the Jews.

Question 1b Some qualities are: mercy and grace (he does not judge or wipe out his people); he stays involved with his people; holiness; he is communicative, clearly stating his expectations and objectives.

Question 2 The nations are getting a wrong picture of God and this further hinders them from being reconciled to him. This breaks God's heart.

Question 3 The purpose of this question is to help people reflect on the amazing privilege and responsibility that we have as God's people. God has chosen us to be coworkers with him, to accomplish his ultimate purpose for all of creation. Answers like, "Beats me! I don't understand why God would take such a risk with me!" are fine.

Question 5 Idols of today are both external (such as "money") and internal (such as "my demand for sexual satisfaction"). The exercises which defined "flesh" in Session One should help people to connect the struggles in their hearts with idolatry. The next few questions will also help them make this connection.

Questions 6 and 7 It is extremely important that the tone of the group is one that is gracious, inviting people to look at their hearts without condemnation. The whole point of this exercise is to help group members see that God is actively working to free us from idols. If we hide them from him, we will remain in bondage.

Question 8 The promise is one which Christians receive when they put their faith in Christ for salvation. It is for cleansing from sin, freedom from idols, the receiving of a new heart, and even receiving God's Spirit. It is the work of this Spirit whom we have fully received in salvation to keep on cleansing, freeing, and renewing our heart.

Question 9 A possible paraphrase: The Spirit will instruct us and empower us to do God's will.

Question 10 Again, the point here is to help people realize that God is in them and for them. He is offering them whatever they need to escape ungodliness and to bear good fruit. Condemnation, that is, beating yourself over the head with thoughts like *I'm so stu-*

pid to still struggle after all God did for me; I'm hopeless, is simply playing into the enemy's hand.

Question 12 It is vital for people to grasp the fact that grace is the present, active work of God which releases truth and power in each of us to do his will. He has cleansed us from sin and made it possible for his Holy Spirit to come to live within us individually, so that he can teach and empower us to say "no" to sin and "yes" to God.

Responding to God

This session will probably have touched some very personal issues. It may be best to pray in twos and threes in the group, and also encourage people to talk to the Lord alone, or pray with a trusted friend if appropriate.

session three

Grasping His Love

Isaiah 53:1–9

Purpose: To introduce consideration of the cross into the process of looking at sin and flesh, so that the participants are reminded of God's great love for them, his hatred of evil, and all he did to cleanse and free us from it.

Engaging the Text

Question 1 Possible statements: He had no beauty, no majesty, no power or position. He was simple, plain, possibly unattractive. He was a reject; the object of hatred. He was ignored. He was hated.

Question 2a We have infirmities. We have sorrows. We suffer. We have transgressions. We have iniquities (the flesh, which are the ways, habits, and patterns of living that trap us in sin). We have gone astray. We have gone our own way.

Question 2b Jesus experienced sorrow, grief, suffering, rejection, shame, even death.

Question 2c Jesus took on our sickness, our sorrows, and even our punishment from God. He was crucified for our sins and our flesh.

Question 4 The point of this question is to help people think further about what it cost Jesus to make it possible for us to be reconciled to God.

Question 5 The discussion here should center on the evil of sin and the holiness and justice of God.

Question 7 The discussion here should be on the fact that grace to forgive sin is not cheap. Jesus suffered the wrath of God because of it. The significant point of this session is that if we kept in mind what Jesus went through to set us free from sin, we would be less likely to sin in a casual, "in-your-face" way.

Question 9 The flesh is rooted in lies about God or ourselves. A better understanding of God and how much he loves us is vital in undermining these lies and strengthening people against sin.

Question 10 The sidebar "The Way to Freedom" will help in explaining this process. It is important to understand that the flesh is not just a vague power pushing people beyond their control, but it is a complex system of lies enmeshed in feelings that people choose to act on. As we are strengthened with truth, the lies lose their power. Key in the process of crucifying flesh is listening to God's Spirit, who always speaks truth and helps us to understand how to specifically crucify the flesh. You might also find it helpful to look at the study guide "Experiencing the Spirit: Living in the Active Presence of God" in this Living Encounters series.

session four

Recognizing the traps
2 Samuel 11:1–12:24

Purpose: To invite participants to look more closely at how people get trapped in sin, so that they can recognize the trap before they fall into it. God's grace actively works to keep people from sinning. If they do sin, he works to move them toward the cross to freely receive his forgiveness.

Engaging the Text

Question 1 The point is that Uriah is an honorable man, even a friend of David's.

Question 2 David's sins include:

v. 1: As king, he should have gone to war. He chooses to stay home.

vv. 2–3: David keeps on looking at Bathsheba until she has all his attention.

vv. 4–5: Once he knows who she is (her family and her husband), he still sends for her and sleeps with her.

vv. 6–7: There is a war going on, yet David, wanting to cover up his sin, interrupts his commanding general and asks for one of his best men to come home.

v. 13: In the face of Uriah's honoring him as king (v. 9) and Uriah's unselfishness (v. 11), David continues in his deception. In desperation, he gets Uriah drunk so he will sleep with his wife. (Uriah still refuses to be selfish.)

vv. 14–15: David then uses his executive power to order another man to manipulate the situation so that Uriah as well as other innocent men will die, in an effort to keep his sin hidden.

v. 25: Even when David hears that his army is defeated and that Uriah and several others have lost their lives, he does not repent but sends a hypocritical response.

Question 3 From the list of sins identified in Question 2, help people to think through choices David makes along the way and to brainstorm other kinds of choices he could have made. Note that most of the ways out of his situation are simple. He has to work very hard to execute his sin and cover it up.

Question 5 This should lead to discussion about the healthiness of having people in our lives who know us and feel free to talk to us about things they see in us which concern them. Some people may not have these kinds of friends and may feel awkward about this. But it could be helpful to consider *(part b)* why they do not have such friends and what they can do to change that.

Question 9 It is important for people to understand that not all bad things that happen in our lives are the results of our sin. For example, many babies die, but it does not mean that each death is an act of God because of someone's sin. On the other hand, when we do persist in sin, God sometimes disciplines us in a manner that will help us learn to respect him and his ways. This is what he does with David.

session five

Responding in Grace

2 Corinthians 11:1–12:10

Purpose: To help people see that God's grace is available to them in the midst of all kinds of hardship, and to invite them to receive that grace, even in their present circumstances.

Engaging the Text

Question 3 The point of this question is to help the participants see that Paul is being treated badly by the Corinthians. He does not deserve their fickleness. They betray him, are disloyal to him, and doubt his integrity.

Question 6 It is important to be aware that some people may be in an abusive relationship and in need of more help to deal with the situation, both emotionally and practically. The sidebar "Letting Go of the Past" can help to explain this further.

Question 9 Grace is God's active work in our hearts. He speaks the truth, reminds us of who he is, who we are, and what life is ultimately about. This strengthens us so that our attitudes and actions are rooted in him and his truth, not in the circumstances.

Question 10 Paul speaks of himself in the third person: "I knew a man." This is simply a literary device to draw attention away from himself and on to the point that he is making.

Question 11 Paul reports that he was first upset about the "thorn." He resisted it. He repeatedly asked God to get rid of it. He never mistook the evil of it as coming from God, understanding that evil is from Satan. He simply recognized in the end that God had a good reason for him to continue to live with it. He received God's grace—his active truth and power—to strengthen himself in the situation, and he let go of his right to live without the thorn.

fINISHING STRONG

Ephesians 6:10–18; Philippians 3:7–14

Purpose: To encourage people to focus on the big picture of what their life is all about, and then to understand God's provision (his armor) to strengthen them against the enemy's attacks and efforts to derail them.

Engaging the Text

Please note that although Questions 5, 6, 8, and 9 have two parts each, they do not require long answers. (Question 4 is also simply an observation question to help participants get involved with the text.) This section should therefore take no longer to work through than the other studies.

Question 1 In the previous verses of Ephesians, Paul has laid the foundation of what it means to be "in Christ." Even though Christ is in the believer through his Spirit and the believer is in Christ, we don't always live out of this reality. Thus Paul prays in Ephesians 1:18–23 and 3:16–19 that our eyes would be open to his provision within us. Here in 6:10, Paul is exhorting Christians to receive what God provides to strengthen us.

Question 2 The aim is simply to provoke some thought and discussion in the group about what kinds of things strengthen a person's heart.

Question 3 Most difficult situations are complex. It is important that the participants do not simply overlook the human factor. People do sin against us. The wrong needs to be acknowledged and dealt with when necessary. It is not to be ignored. However, Paul wants us to see that more than the human factor is involved. Satan uses a person's sin as an occasion to further his destructive purposes in our heart or in our relationship with the one who sins against us. Becoming aware that Satan is trying to influence our reactions can help people to resist him and follow the Holy Spirit's leading as they respond.

Question 5   The sidebar "Seeing with New Eyes" gives a helpful explanation of taking hold of truth.

Question 6   Righteousness means right standing with God. There are slightly different perspectives concerning this question. However, in practice, most would respond in the same way, the reality being that Christians are righteous through their faith in Jesus, and Jesus died for our sins, thus opening the way for the Holy Spirit to be given to us. "Putting on righteousness" can simply mean that we live in the awareness that the Holy Spirit really lives in us. This can make us think twice before sinning. However, Christians do sin. When we do, it is crucial to acknowledge that sin before God, repent, and receive his free, gracious provision against sin. This closes the door so that the enemy cannot gain any foothold in our hearts by condemning us, driving us toward a cover-up, or leading us into repeated sin.

Question 7   Point out that we are to be ready to respond in reconciliation, even before trouble comes.

Question 8   For further study and discussion on this topic, see the study guide "Experiencing the Spirit: Living in the Active Presence of God" in this Living Encounters Series.

Question 11 Paul's mission statement could be something like: "I define myself and my success by that which deepens my relationship with Christ." Or "My attitudes and actions must flow out of receiving all Christ died to give me."

Question 12 It is important to remember that we are "God's workmanship, created in Christ Jesus to do good works" (Ephesians 2:10); that is, God has been and still is at work in and through us to do good. Our life's purpose can be accomplished by continuing to interact with God, receiving his provisions to face life's challenges.

If you know the Lord, you have already heard his voice—it is that inner leading that brought you to him in the first place. Jesus always checked with his Father (John 8:26–29), and so should we; hearing the voice of the heavenly Father is a basic right of every child of God. The following are a number of ways of fine-tuning this experience:

1

Hearing God's voice is possible for you!

Don't make guidance complicated. It's actually hard not to hear God if you really want to please and obey him! If you stay humble, he promises to guide you (Proverbs 16:9). Here are three simple steps to help in hearing his voice:

- *Submit* to his lordship. Ask him to help you silence your own thoughts and desires and the opinions of others that may be filling your mind (2 Corinthians 10:5). Even though you have been given a good mind to use, right now you want to hear the thoughts of the Lord, who has the *best* mind (Proverbs 3:5–6).
- *Resist* the enemy, in case he is trying to deceive you at this moment. Use the authority that Jesus Christ has given you to silence the voice of the enemy (Ephesians 6:10–20; James 4:7).
- *Expect* your loving heavenly Father to speak to you. After asking your question, wait for him to answer. He will (Exodus 33:11; Psalm 69:13; John 10:27).

2

God speaks in different ways

Allow God to speak to you in the way he chooses. Don't try to dictate to him concerning the guidance methods you prefer. He is Lord—you are his servant (1 Samuel 3:9). So listen with a yielded heart; there is a direct link between yield-edness and hearing. He may choose to speak to you through *his Word*. This could come in your daily reading of the Bible, or he could guide you to a particular verse (Psalm 119:105). He may speak to you through an *audible voice* (Exodus 3:4), through dreams (Matthew 2), or through *visions* (Isaiah 6:1; Revelation 1:12–17). But probably the most common way is through the quiet *inner voice* (Isaiah 30:21).

3	**Acknowledge your sin before God**	Confess any sin. A clean heart is necessary if you want to hear God (Psalm 66:18).
4	**Revisit the scene of God's guidance**	Use the Axhead Principle (see 2 Kings 6). If you seem to have lost your way, go back to the last time you knew the sharp, cutting edge of God's voice. Then obey. The key question is, "Have you obeyed the last thing God has told you to do?"
5	**God can and will speak to you!**	Get your own leading. God will use others to confirm your guidance, but you should also hear from him directly. It can be dangerous to rely on others to get the word of the Lord for you (1 Kings 13).
6	**God will make it clear in his time**	Don't talk about your guidance until God gives you permission to do so. Sometimes this happens immediately; at other times there is a delay. The main purpose of waiting is to avoid four pitfalls: *pride*—because God has spoken to you; *presumption*—by speaking before you have full understanding; *missing God's timing and method*; and *bringing confusion to others*, who also need prepared hearts (Ecclesiastes 3:7; Mark 5:19; Luke 9:36).
7	**Be alert to the signs God provides**	Use the Wise-Men Principle (see Matthew 2). Just as the wise men individually followed the star and were all led to the same Christ, so God will often use two or more spiritually sensitive people to *confirm* what he is telling you (2 Corinthians 13:1).
8	**Discern true guidance from false guidance**	Beware of counterfeits. Of course you have heard of a counterfeit dollar bill. But have you ever heard of a counterfeit paper bag? No. Why not? Because only things of value are worth counterfeiting. Satan has a counterfeit of everything of God that is possible for him to copy (Exodus 7:22; Acts 8:9–11). Counterfeit guidance comes, for example, through Ouija boards, seances, fortune-telling, and astrology (Leviticus 19:26; 20:6; 2 Kings 21:6). The guidance of the Holy Spirit leads you closer to Jesus and into true freedom. Satan's guidance leads you away from God into bondage. One key test for true guidance: Does your leading follow biblical principles? The Holy Spirit never contradicts the Word of God. Confess any sin. A clean heart is necessary if you want to hear God (Psalm 66:18).

9 **Yield your heart completely to the Lord**

Opposition from humans is sometimes guidance from God (Acts 21:10–14). The important thing again is yieldedness to the Lord (Daniel 6:6–23; Acts 4:18–21). Rebellion is never of God, but sometimes he asks us to step away from our elders in a way that is not rebellion but part of his plan. Trust that he will show your heart the difference.

10 **God will reveal your calling**

Every follower of Jesus has a unique ministry (Romans 12; 1 Corinthians 12; Ephesians 4:11–13; 1 Peter 4:10–11). The more you seek to hear God's voice in detail, the more effective you will be in your own calling. Guidance is not a game—it is serious business where we learn *what* God wants us to do and *how* he wants us to do it. The will of God is doing and saying the right thing in the right place, with the right people at the right time and in the right sequence, under the right leadership, using the right method with the right attitude of heart.

11 **Stay in constant communication with God**

Practice hearing God's voice and it becomes easier. It's like picking up the phone and recognizing the voice of your best friend . . . you know that voice because you have heard it so many times before. Compare the young Samuel with the older man Samuel (1 Samuel 3:4–7; 8:7–10; 12:11–18).

12 **God wants a relationship with you!**

Relationship is the most important reason for hearing the voice of the Lord. God is not only infinite, but personal. If you don't have communication, you don't have a personal relationship with him. True guidance is getting closer to the Guide. We grow to know the Lord better as he speaks to us; as we listen to him and obey him, we make his heart glad (Exodus 33:11; Matthew 7:24–27).

Loren Cunningham © 1984

1 Praise God for who he is, and for the privilege of engaging in the same wonderful ministry as the Lord Jesus (Hebrews 7:25). Praise God for the privilege of cooperating with him in the affairs of humankind through prayer.

2 Make sure your heart is clean before God by having given the Holy Spirit time to convict, should there be any unconfessed sin (Psalm 66:18; 139:23–24).

3 Acknowledge that you can't really pray without the direction and energy of the Holy Spirit (Romans 8:26). Ask God to utterly control you by his Spirit, receive by faith the reality that he does, and thank him (Ephesians 5:18).

4 Deal aggressively with the enemy. Come against him in the all-powerful name of the Lord Jesus Christ and with the "sword of the Spirit"—the Word of God (Ephesians 6:17; James 4:7).

5 Die to your own imaginations, desires, and burdens for what you feel you should pray about (Proverbs 3:5–6; 28:26; Isaiah 55:8).

6 Praise God now in faith for the remarkable prayer meeting you're going to have. He's a remarkable God, and he will do something consistent with his character.

7 Wait before God in silent expectancy, listening for his direction (Psalm 62:5; 81:11–13; Micah 7:7).

8 In obedience and faith, utter what God brings to your mind, believing (John 10:27). Keep asking God for direction, expecting him to give it to you. He will (Psalm 32:8). Make sure you don't move to the next subject until you've given God time to discharge all he wants to say regarding this burden—especially when praying in a group. Be encouraged by the lives of Moses, Daniel, Paul, and Anna, knowing that God gives revelation to those who make intercession a way of life.

9	If possible, have your Bible with you should God want to give you direction or confirmation from it (Psalm 119:105).
10	When God ceases to bring things to your mind for which to pray, finish by praising and thanking him for what he has done, reminding yourself of Romans 11:36: "For from him and through him and to him are all things. To him be the glory forever! Amen."

A WARNING: God knows the weakness of the human heart toward pride. If we speak of what God has revealed and done in intercession, it may lead to committing this sin. God shares his secrets with those who are able to keep them. There may come a time when he definitely prompts us to share, but unless this happens, we should remain silent: "The disciples kept this to themselves, and told no one at that time what they had seen" (Luke 9:36). "Mary treasured up all these things and pondered them in her heart" (Luke 2:19).

Joy Dawson © 1985

World Map

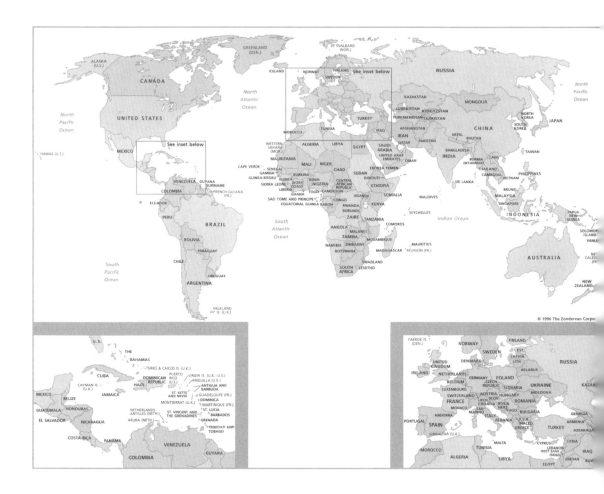

© 1996 The Zondervan Corpo...

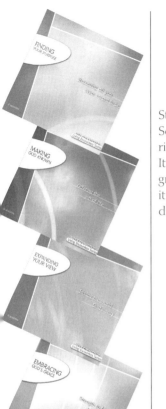

stay CONNECTED!

Living Encounters Series
Youth With A Mission

Styled after Youth With A Mission's (YWAM) successful Discipleship Training School (DTS), the Living Encounters series draws on YWAM's years of experience and expertise in training people of all ages for international ministry. Its unique, life-changing approach to Bible study will expand your small group's paradigm of Christianity . . . liberate its spiritual passion . . . and fill it with the joy and spiritual vigor that come from following an unpredictable, radical, and totally amazing risen Lord.

Experiencing the Spirit: *Living in the Active Presence of God* 0-310-22706-2
Seeing Jesus: *The Father Made Visible* 0-310-22707-0
Encountering God: *The God You've Always Wanted to Know* 0-310-22708-9
Building Relationships: *Connections for Life* 0-310-22709-7
Embracing God's Grace: *Strength to Face Life's Challenges* 0-310-22229-X
Expanding Your View: *Seeing the World God's Way* 0-310-22704-6
Making God Known: *Offering the Gift of Life* 0-310-22703-8
Finding Your Purpose: *Becoming All You Were Meant to Be* 0-310-22702-X

Look for Living Encounters at your local Christian bookstore.
ZondervanPublishingHouse

about Youth With a Mission

The Heart of Youth With A Mission

Youth With A Mission (YWAM) is an international movement of Christians from many denominations dedicated to presenting Jesus Christ personally to this generation, to mobilizing as many as possible to help in this task, and to training and equipping believers for their part in fulfilling the Great Commission. As Christians of God's Kingdom, we are called to love, worship, and obey our Lord, to love and serve his body, the Church, and to present the whole gospel for the whole man throughout the whole world.

We in Youth With A Mission believe that the Bible is God's inspired and authoritative Word, revealing that Jesus Christ is God's Son; that man is created in God's image; and that he created us to have eternal life through Jesus Christ; that although all men have sinned and come short of God's glory, God has made salvation possible through the death on the cross and resurrection of Jesus Christ.

We believe that repentance, faith, love, and obedience are fitting responses to God's initiative of grace toward us; that God desires all men to be saved and to come to the knowledge of truth; and that the Holy Spirit's power is demonstrated in and through us for the accomplishing of Christ's last commandment: "Go into all the world and preach the good news to all creation" (Mark 16:15).

How Youth With A Mission Works

YWAM embraces three modes of action—ways which we believe God has given us to be a part of the goal of taking the gospel to all the world:

Evangelism — spreading God's message.
Training — preparing workers to reach others.
Mercy Ministries — showing God's love through practical assistance.

Youth With A Mission has a particular mandate for mobilizing and championing the ministry potential of young people. But our worldwide missions force also includes thousands of older people from all kinds of social, cultural, ethnic, and professional backgrounds. Our staff of 12,000 includes people from more than 135 nations and ranges from relatively new Christians to veteran pastors and missionaries.

We are committed to a lifestyle of dependence on God for guidance, financial provision, and holy living. We also affirm a lifestyle of worship, prayer, godly character, hospitality, generosity, servant leadership, team ministry, personal responsibility, and right relationships with one another and our families.

Because of its visionary calling, YWAM does new things in new ways where new initiatives are required. We seek to build bridges among Christian leaders, partnering with local churches and missions for completion of the Great Commission. Annually, over 35,000 people from various churches take part in YWAM's short-term outreach projects.

Teams from Youth With A Mission have now ministered in every country of the world and have ministry centers in 142 nations, but the work is far from complete. We welcome all who want to know God and make him known to join with us in finishing the task — to "make disciples of all nations" (Matthew 28:19).

for more information

For more information about YWAM, please contact YWAM Publishing to obtain YWAM's *Go Manual*, an annual directory of YWAM's addresses and training and service opportunities (send $5 to cover costs), or write one of our field offices for more information. Note: Please mention the Living Encounters Bible study series in your request for information.

YWAM Field Offices

Youth With A Mission
(The Americas Office)
P.O. Box 4600
Tyler, TX 75712 U.S.A.
1–903–882–5591

Youth With A Mission
(Europe, Middle East, & Africa Office)
Highfield Oval, Harpenden
Herts. AL5 4BX
England, U.K.
(44) 1582–463–300

Youth With A Mission
(Pacific & Asia Office)
P.O. Box 7
Mitchell, A.C.T. 2911
Australia
(61) 6–241–5500

YWAM International DTS
(Discipleship Training School) Centre
PF 608
Budapest 62
1399 Hungary
100726.1773@compuserve.com

YWAM Publishing

P.O. Box 55787
Seattle, WA 98155 U.S.A.
Phone: 1–800–922–2143 (U.S. only) or
1–425–771–1153
Fax: 1 425 775 2383
E-mail address:
75701.2772@compuserve.com
Web page:
www.ywampublishing.com

DISCOVER YOUR PERSONAL PATH TOWARD INTIMACY WITH GOD

CHRISTIAN GROWTH STUDY BIBLE
New International Version

If you've enjoyed this YWAM study guide, you'll love this YWAM study Bible! The *Christian Growth Study Bible* is designed to help you cultivate heart-to-heart closeness with God. The kind you've longed for and God created you for. A dynamic, growing relationship so vital and life-changing that you can't keep it to yourself—you've got to tell the world about it and help others discover the greatness of your heavenly Father.

Knowing God and Making Him Known is the heartbeat of the *Christian Growth Study Bible*. It's also the heartbeat of Youth With A Mission (YWAM). Which is why this Bible's study program is modeled after YWAM's proven approach in their Discipleship Training Schools. At last, here's a study Bible with a 30-path program that will help you take the uncertainty out of your Christian growth. It helps you determine where you are on the path toward maturity—and helps remove the guesswork about where to go from there.

This *Christian Growth Study Bible* will be an invaluable tool for you to use with your Living Encounters Bible study series, giving you further help on the topics you will be exploring.

Hardcover	ISBN 0-310-91809X
	ISBN 0-310-918138 Indexed
Softcover	ISBN 0-310-918103
Black Bonded Leather	ISBN 0-310-91812X
	ISBN 0-310-918154 Indexed
Burgundy Bonded Leather	ISBN 0-310-918111
	ISBN 0-310-918146 Indexed

We want to hear from you. Please send your comments about this
book to us in care of the address below. Thank you.

ZondervanPublishingHouse
Grand Rapids, Michigan 49530
http://www.zondervan.com